# A Short, Illustrated History of
# MEDICINE

John C. Miles   Rita Petruccioli

**W**
**FRANKLIN WATTS**
LONDON • SYDNEY

# CONTENTS

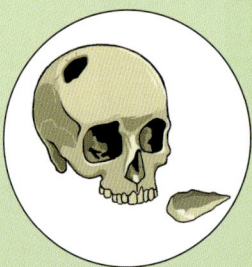
4-5
PREHISTORIC MEDICINE

6-7
ANCIENT GREEK AND ROMAN MEDICINE

8-9
CHINESE AND ISLAMIC MEDICINE

14-15
CIRCULATION

16-17
SAILORS AND SCURVY

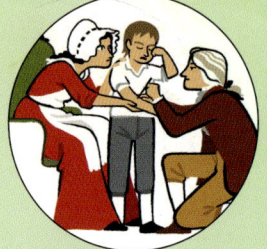
18-19
SMALLPOX AND INOCULATION

24-25
LOUIS PASTEUR AND VACCINES

26-27
ANTISEPTIC SURGERY

28-29
PSYCHIATRY

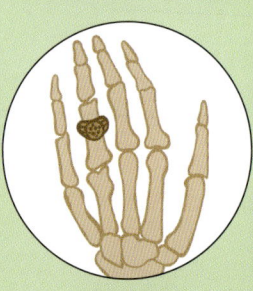
30-31
RÖNTGEN AND X-RAYS

36-37
INSULIN

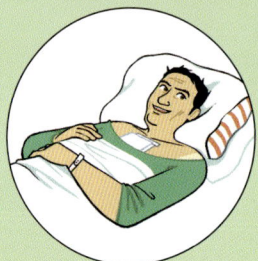
38-39
FIRST HEART TRANSPLANT

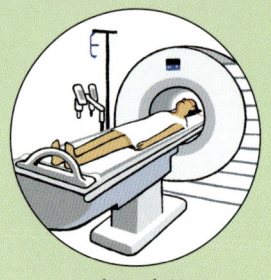
40-41
IMAGING

42-43
JOINT REPLACEMENT SURGERY

**10-11**
**NEW THEORIES**

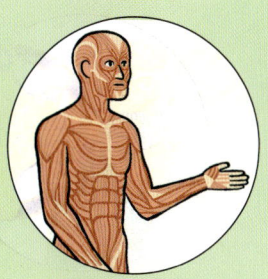
**12-13**
**DISSECTION AND ANATOMY**

**20-21**
**CHOLERA**

**22-23**
**ANAESTHETICS**

**32-33**
**MAGIC BULLETS**

**34-35**
**ANTIBIOTICS - A CHANCE DISCOVERY**

**44-45**
**GENETIC THERAPY AND THE FUTURE**

**46-47**
**GLOSSARY/ FURTHER INFORMATION**

**48**
**PLACES TO VISIT/INDEX**

Franklin Watts
First published in Great Britain in 2020 by
The Watts Publishing Group
Copyright © The Watts Publishing Group, 2020

All rights reserved.

HB ISBN: 978 1 4451 6913 2
PB ISBN: 978 1 4451 6914 9

Series Editor: Amy Pimperton
Series Designer: Lisa Peacock
Illustrations by Rita Petruccioli

Printed in China

Franklin Watts
An imprint of
Hachette Children's Group
Part of The Watts Publishing Group
Carmelite House
50 Victoria Embankment
London EC4Y 0DZ
An Hachette UK Company

www.hachette.co.uk
www.franklinwatts.co.uk

The facts and statistics in this book were correct at the time of printing.

The websites (URLS) included in this book were valid at the time of going to press. However, it is possible that the contents or addresses may have changed since the publication of this book. No responsibility for any such changes can be accepted by either the author or the Publisher.

# PREHISTORIC MEDICINE

Humans have always suffered from a wide range of diseases and injuries. Thousands of years ago no one wrote things down, so today's historians have to rely on archaeological evidence, such as human remains, to support theories about prehistoric medicine.

Evidence suggests that average life expectancy was low – between 25 and 40 years. People suffered from osteoarthritis, caused by moving heavy objects, as well as broken bones. In years when there were not enough animals to hunt, people experienced malnutrition. Women probably lived shorter lives than men because many died in childbirth.

Prehistoric humans would have used plants, such as aloe vera, to treat injuries and illnesses. Plant material rots easily, so it's hard to find evidence for what plants were used in prehistory. Early plant-based medicine must have included much trial and error, sometimes with fatal consequences.

*Prehistoric humans discovered the medical benefits of plants, such as aloe vera.*

One ancient surgical procedure for which evidence does exist is trepanning. The scalp was cut, peeled back and a hole slowly scraped into the skull with a sharp flint to expose brain tissue. Historians aren't certain why this 'surgery' was performed – perhaps it was to let evil spirits out in cases of severe headaches or epilepsy. What is clear is that people survived the operation, as some trepanned skulls show evidence of bone growing back around the wound.

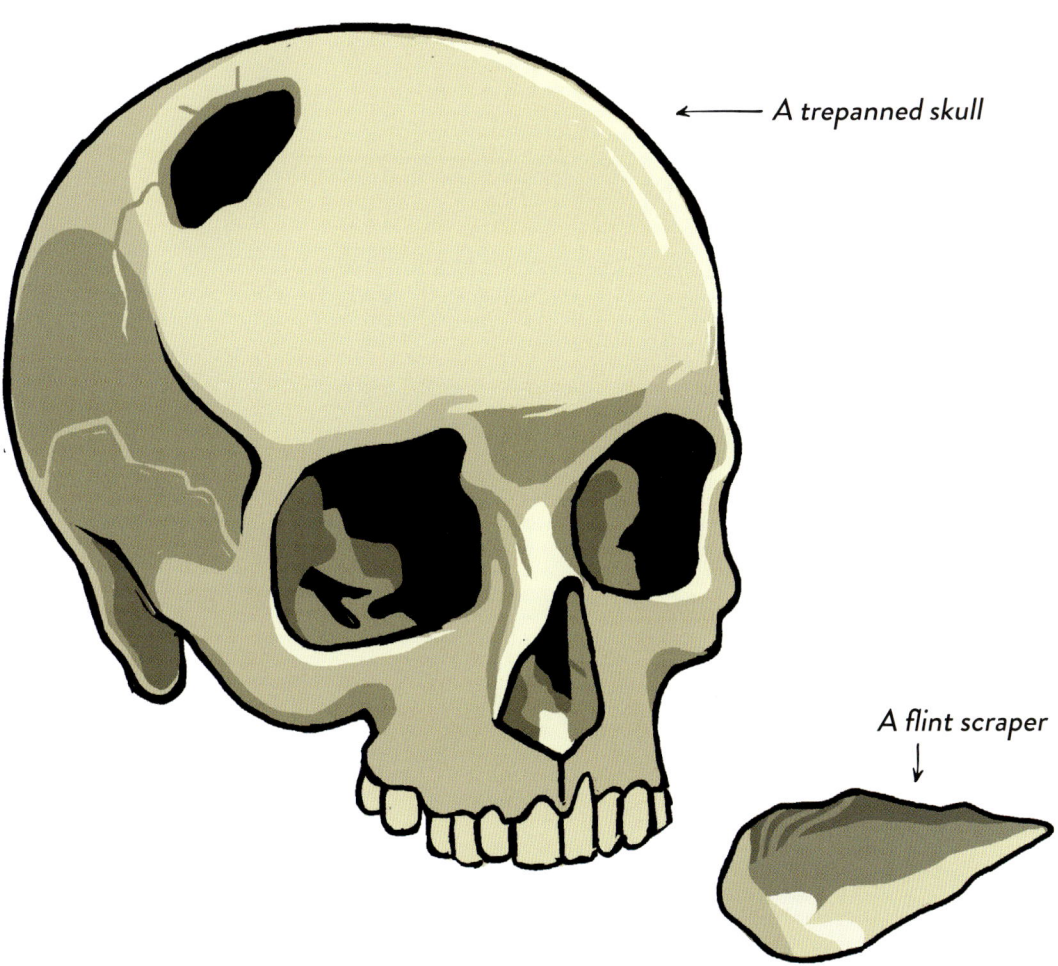

*A trepanned skull*

*A flint scraper*

It is only in the last few centuries that doctors and scientists have made medical discoveries that mean we understand how the body is put together and what causes many diseases. This book is the story of some of these key moments in medical history.

# ANCIENT GREEK AND ROMAN MEDICINE

The thinkers of the ancient Greek and Roman worlds developed ideas about illness, medicine and the body, many of which were held on to by the doctors of later cultures for hundreds of years.

Early Greeks viewed illness as a punishment from displeased gods. Doctors used spells and sacrifices to try to cure their patients. Later, doctors such as Hippocrates (c. 460–370 BCE) – founder of an early medical school – believed that four elements or 'humours' existed within the human body. These liquids were blood, phlegm, black bile and yellow bile. If a person was too hot, cold, wet or dry it disturbed the balance of these humours and caused disease.

*Hippocrates*

*Each of the humours relates to an 'element'.\* Clockwise from top, these are: air (blood), water (phlegm), earth (black bile) and fire (yellow bile).*

\* In chemistry, an element is a chemical substance, such as hydrogen or carbon. Air, water, earth and fire aren't true elements.

Biological factors, such as inhaling bad air, could also affect the humours. Doctors focused on finding ways of rebalancing the body's humours, for example, by drawing blood from a vein or prescribing a herbal remedy, to restore health.

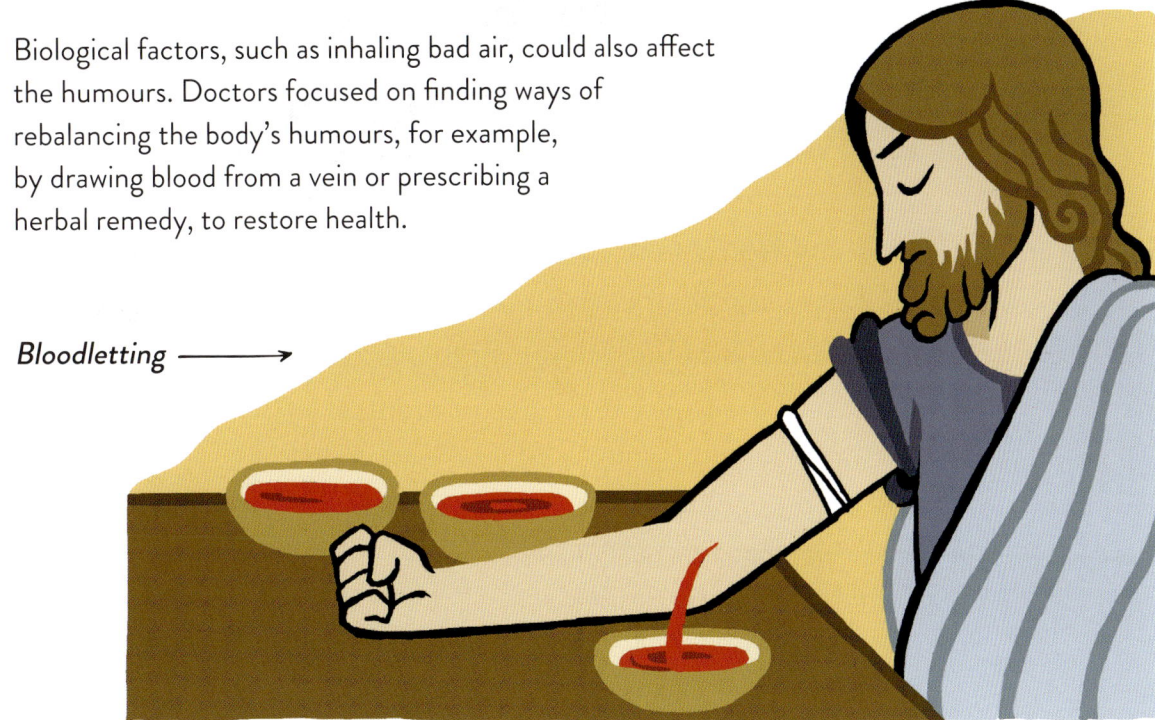

*Bloodletting* ⟶

The ancient Romans incorporated many ideas and techniques from Greek medicine into their own. The surviving number of bronze surgical instruments shows that Roman doctors were skilled at surgery. They could deal with battle wounds as well as complicated childbirth.

## Aelius Galenus

Known as Galen (c. CE 129–210) he was born in the Greek city of Pergamon (present-day Turkey), but settled in Rome. He travelled widely, sampling the medical practices of many different cultures. Galen, too, was a great believer in the idea of the four humours and studied anatomy by dissecting apes. His ideas dominated Western medicine for more than 1,300 years.

*Aelius Galenus*

# CHINESE AND ISLAMIC MEDICINE

While Greek and Roman doctors worked with the four humours, physicians in China used their own medical techniques well established for centuries. Hundreds of years later, highly educated doctors of the Islamic world made great strides in medical knowledge.

## CHINESE MEDICINE

Although historians believe medical practices in China date back to the Shang Dynasty (c. 1600–1046 BCE), the first Chinese medical book, *Huangdi Neijing* (*The Yellow Emperor's Classic of Medicine*), dates from approximately 200–300 BCE. The book includes symptoms of various diseases along with possible treatments.

Traditional Chinese medicine favours a holistic approach to health, meaning that doctors treat the body, mind and spirit of the patient using a variety of methods, including herbs, acupuncture, exercise and massage. These aim to balance the flow of life energy, or *qi* (chi) within the human body.

*Huangdi (The Yellow Emperor)*

*The yin-yang symbol represents balance, which is a key concept in many aspects of Chinese culture, including medicine.*

## ISLAMIC MEDICINE

During the time of the Islamic 'golden age' – from the 8th to 14th century CE – centres of learning, such as Baghdad and Bukhara (now in modern Iraq and Uzbekistan), produced doctors with skills far in advance of doctors in Western Europe. Islamic medicine adopted the medical practices of earlier cultures, such as Greece, Rome and India, then built on these to make advances in areas such as eye diseases.

Persian philosopher, astronomer and physician Ibn Sīnā (c. CE 980–1037) – also known as Avicenna – lived in Central Asia and in what is now Iran. A brilliant thinker, Ibn Sīnā qualified as a doctor at the age of 18 and worked for various Islamic rulers. He wrote *The Book of Healing* and *The Canon of Medicine*, which remained in use in Western universities until the 17th century.

Ibn Sīnā ⟶

# NEW THEORIES

Swiss doctor Theophrastus Bombastus von Hohenheim (1493 or 1494–1541), known as Paracelsus, was a physician and chemist. He pioneered new theories about illness when the practice of medicine was still firmly based on the ideas of ancient Greece and Rome.

Paracelsus trained and worked as a military surgeon. At the time, physicians followed the theories of ancient thinkers such as Hippocrates and Galen – the belief that disease was caused by an imbalance of humours within the body (see pages 6–7). Paracelsus questioned this, suggesting that disease was in fact caused by things from outside the body attacking it.

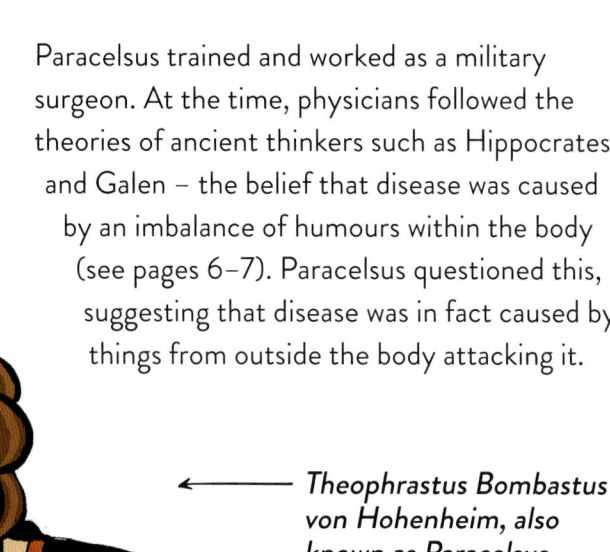

*Theophrastus Bombastus von Hohenheim, also known as Paracelsus*

## Nickname

It is thought that Bombastus von Hohenheim's friends gave him the name Paracelsus – which means 'above Celsus' – to signify that his thinking had moved on from the ancient world, as personified by the Greek philosopher Celsus.

Paracelsus was an early believer in antisepsis and keeping wounds clean to allow the body to heal itself. He also studied the disease syphilis, which was sweeping through Europe. This hideous illness produces painful oozing sores, a rash of blisters, the collapse of features – such as the nose – and, eventually, insanity and death. Paracelsus observed that syphilis could be passed on by sexual contact and could also be inherited by a baby from its infected mother.

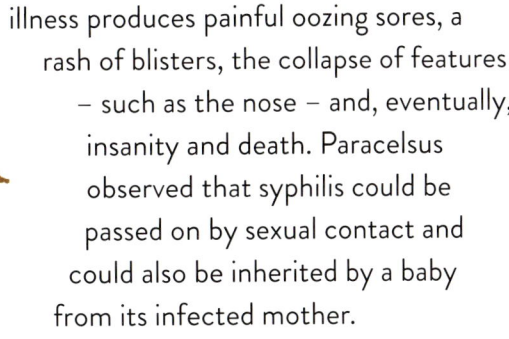

*Syphilis produces a painful skin rash.*

A skilled chemist, Paracelsus experimented with using minerals and chemicals as medicines. He reintroduced the painkiller opium to Europe and correctly prescribed iron for patients with 'poor blood', or anaemia. He discovered the element zinc and suggested that some illnesses could be caused by an imbalance of minerals within the body.

*Opium is a pain-relieving drug developed from poppy plants. It also makes patients feel sleepy.*

# DISSECTION AND ANATOMY

Before the work of Flemish doctor Andreas Vesalius (1514–64), people knew little about what actually went on inside the human body. Through careful dissection, observation and comparison, this brilliant doctor made a huge contribution to anatomical knowledge.

In 1537 Vesalius became professor of anatomy and surgery at the University of Padua, Italy. At the time, teaching anatomy involved studying Galen (see pages 6–7) and other ancient writers before watching a surgeon dissect the bodies of animals.

A talented surgeon, Vesalius preferred to conduct this work himself. But believing that the best way to study human anatomy was to dissect humans, he worked with the cadavers (dead bodies) of executed criminals, carefully recording bones, muscles and organs. He commissioned skilled artists to produce accurate and detailed diagrams of his results.

*Andreas Vesalius (second from left) teaches students during a human dissection*

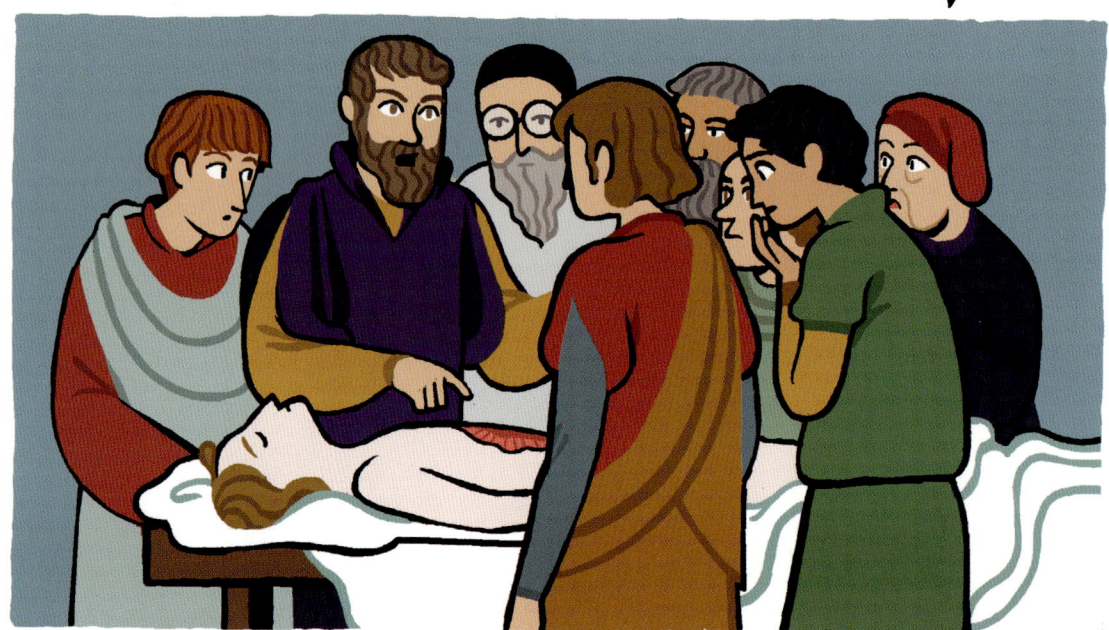

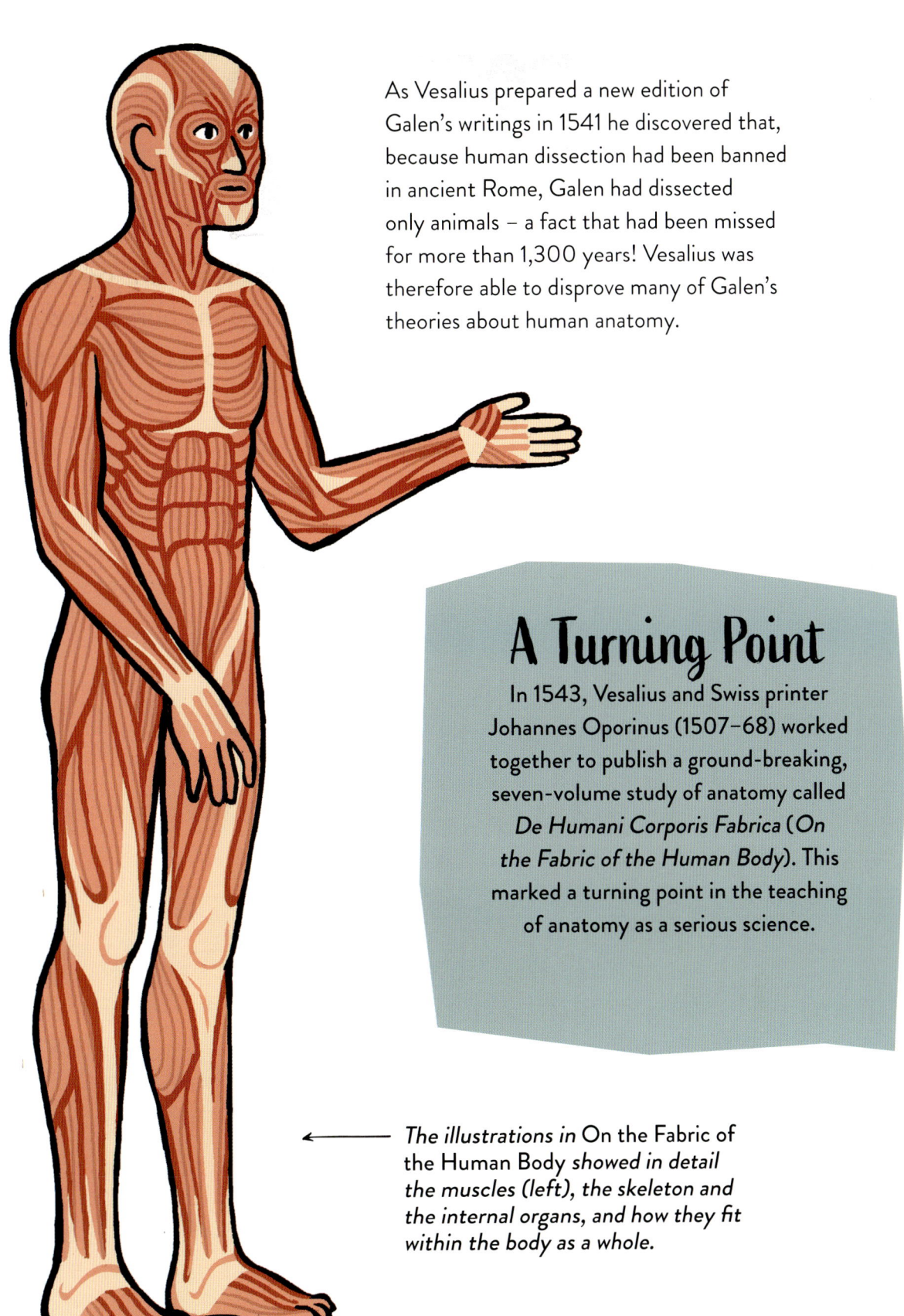

As Vesalius prepared a new edition of Galen's writings in 1541 he discovered that, because human dissection had been banned in ancient Rome, Galen had dissected only animals – a fact that had been missed for more than 1,300 years! Vesalius was therefore able to disprove many of Galen's theories about human anatomy.

## A Turning Point

In 1543, Vesalius and Swiss printer Johannes Oporinus (1507–68) worked together to publish a ground-breaking, seven-volume study of anatomy called *De Humani Corporis Fabrica* (*On the Fabric of the Human Body*). This marked a turning point in the teaching of anatomy as a serious science.

The illustrations in On the Fabric of the Human Body *showed in detail the muscles (left), the skeleton and the internal organs, and how they fit within the body as a whole.*

# CIRCULATION

In 1628 English physician William Harvey (1578–1657) published a book that described how blood circulates. It changed our understanding of how the human body works.

Harvey was a physician to the rich and famous as well as to royalty. He was also an important medical lecturer. His book, *De Moto Cordis* (*On the Action of the Heart*) outlined theories on how the heart works – which was poorly understood at the time – and on how blood circulates around the body.

# Arteries and Veins

Harvey's new theories were at odds with ancient medical writers. Galen (see page 7) believed that there were two circulatory systems; one for blood in the arteries and one for blood in the veins. Harvey's work proved Galen incorrect – the heart pumped all blood around the body with the help of one-way valves inside our veins and arteries. For years Harvey faced criticism and abuse before his ideas were accepted as truth.

*An artery (left) and a vein with a one-way valve (right). Arteries carry oxygenated blood from the heart and lungs; veins carry deoxygenated blood to the heart and lungs.*

Harvey's ideas came from dissections of dead animals and humans, but he also stressed that it was important to observe a living, beating heart in order in order to understand its action – difficult at the time without killing the subject. He observed circulation in humans by tying ligatures (thin cords, tied tightly) around, for example, a person's arm and stopping the blood flow. Above the ligature the arm remained warm and swollen, while the below the cord the limb became cold and pale. When Harvey released the ligature, the lower part of the limb returned to normal as blood flowed into it once more.

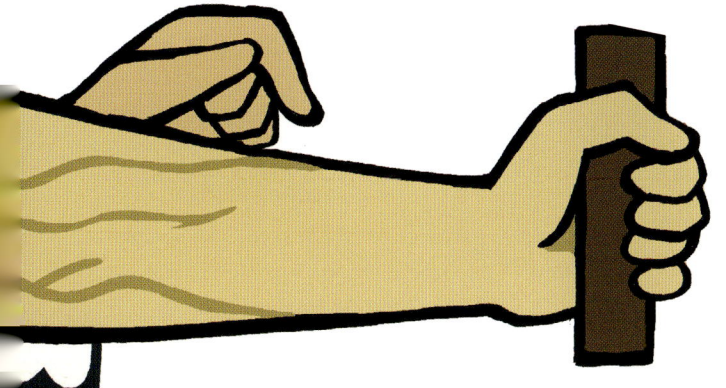

*William Harvey (right) demonstrates his theory of circulation*

# SAILORS AND SCURVY

In 1754 Scottish naval doctor James Lind (1716–94) conducted the world's first-ever clinical trial. His work helped prevent scurvy, a disease caused by a lack of vitamin C.

In the 18th century, ships could be away from home on voyages that lasted for months or years at a time. At sea, a crew's diet consisted of preserved pork or beef, cheese, hard flour biscuit and dried peas. Sailors could get fresh fruit and vegetables when their ships called at ports, but on longer voyages a deadly disease called scurvy often took hold.

Scurvy caused sailors to weaken, with pale skin and sunken eyes. What came next was horrible – teeth dropped out of rotting gums, skin blackened from internal bleeding and long-healed wounds burst open. Left untreated, scurvy led to diarrhoea, kidney failure and death.

The cost of the disease was huge. For example, of the 1,900 sailors on Admiral George Anson's 1740 expedition, up to 1,400 died of scurvy.

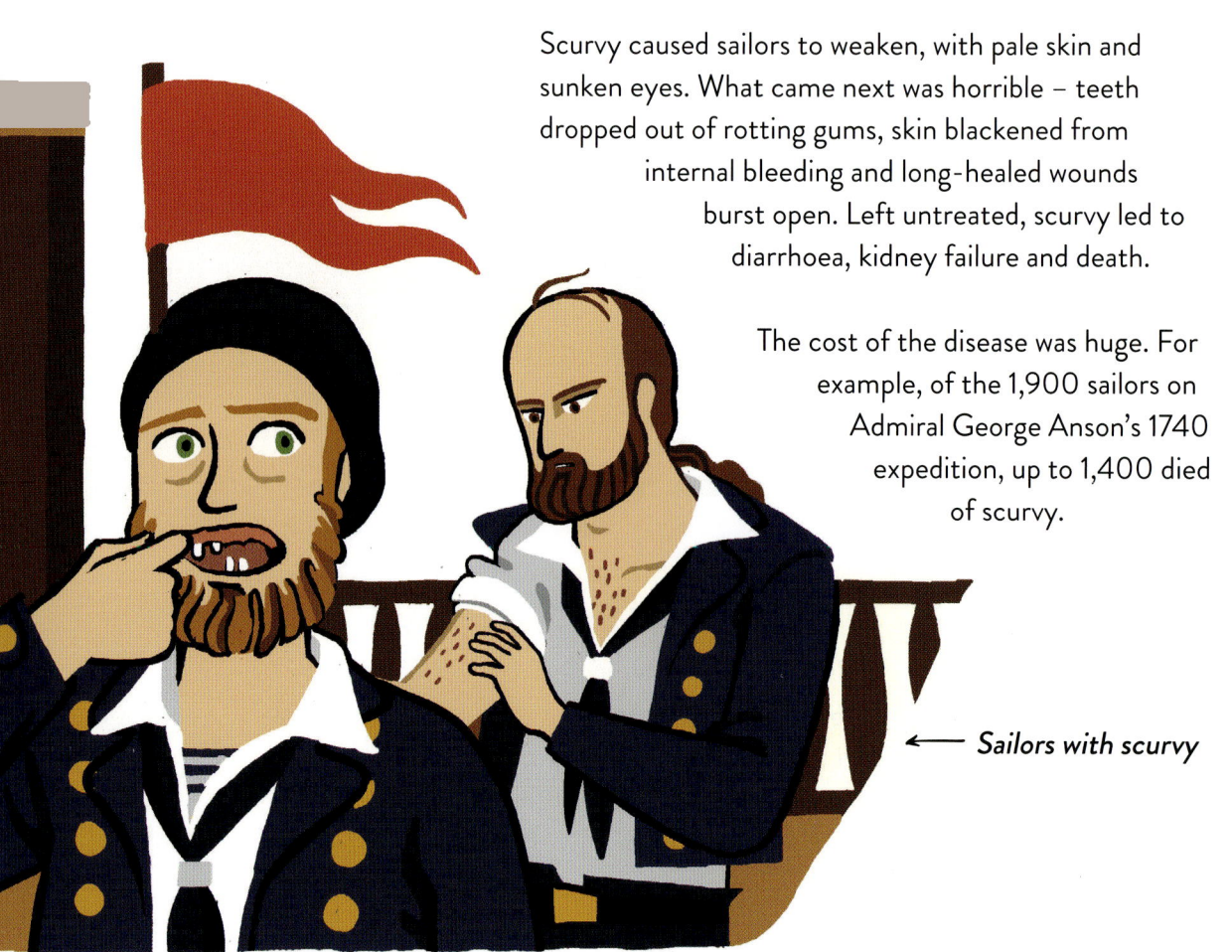

← Sailors with scurvy

James Lind became a naval surgeon and dealt with the effects of scurvy first hand. In 1747 he conducted the world's first clinical trial on HMS *Salisbury* when he tested several possible anti-scurvy remedies on groups of sailors with the disease. One group was given two oranges and one lemon a day. After six days this group had nearly recovered from the illness while the others were still sick.

*James Lind*

## A Daily Dose

Although Lind's achievement was not recognised at the time, his work later helped convince Britain's Royal Navy to issue a daily dose of citrus juice to its sailors. This simple action prevented thousands of deaths in the years that followed.

# SMALLPOX AND INOCULATION

In the 18th century smallpox killed up to 400,000 people every year in Europe alone. English doctor Edward Jenner (1749–1823) pioneered a safe method of inoculation, which gave people immunity to the smallpox virus for life.

Highly contagious, smallpox caused fever, vomiting and a dense skin rash that turned into fluid-filled oozing blisters. The disease killed about 30 per cent of its victims; survivors were left scarred and often blind.

Inoculation – introducing smallpox germs into healthy people to make them immune to further outbreaks – had been practised in China, India and Ottoman Turkey for hundreds of years. Gradually, people in Europe began to be aware of this through contact with the East. But the practice had a high death rate and was usually used only during huge epidemics.

←——— *Edward Jenner*

By the late 18th century people in some rural areas of Europe had observed that milkmaids who caught a mild blistering disease, cowpox, from working with cattle didn't develop smallpox. A country doctor and surgeon, Jenner speculated that if he introduced pus from cowpox blisters into a healthy human through a scratch in the skin, that person would fall ill with cowpox, but would be immune to the much deadlier smallpox.

In May 1796 Jenner put his ideas to the test by inoculating an eight-year-old boy, James Phipps, with pus from a milkmaid's cowpox blisters. Phipps caught cowpox. When he had recovered, Jenner re-inoculated him with material made from the scabs of a smallpox patient. Phipps didn't catch smallpox, proving Jenner correct.

*Edward Jenner inoculates James Phipps*

# Lifesaver

It took years for Jenner's work to be fully accepted but, within a few decades, doctors performed inoculations regularly. It is said that Jenner saved more human lives than any other person; and by 1980 the World Health Organization declared that smallpox had been officially eradicated.

# CHOLERA

Beginning in the 1830s, many cities experienced disastrous cholera epidemics. Cholera is caused by bacteria that live in drinking water polluted by faeces. It causes fever, severe vomiting and uncontrollable diarrhoea. Unable to keep any fluid down or in, victims quickly die of dehydration.

In early Victorian times there were two competing theories of what caused disease. The first, widely accepted, was the 'miasma' theory. This held that diseases were caused by foul air coming from some unpleasant source, such as a graveyard. The second, more radical idea, was the 'germ' theory – that disease was caused by some unseen agent, or 'germ', that had not yet been discovered.

*A cholera bacterium*

John Snow (1813–58) was a doctor who worked in Soho, an overcrowded and dirty district of London. When the area was hit by a severe cholera outbreak in August 1854, Snow carefully mapped where cases occurred, eventually tracing the epidemic to a drinking water pump in Broad Street. A clue came from the local brewery; men who worked there were given beer to drink and stayed healthy.

Snow convinced local authorities to remove the pump's handle, making it unusable, and the epidemic petered out. It later turned out that the pump's water supply had been contaminated by cholera-infected faeces leaking from a nearby cesspit.

*John Snow and the Broad Street pump*

Snow established a clear link between drinking contaminated water and cholera. Although he faced opposition from doctors who continued to stick to the miasma theory, Snow's vital work pointed the way towards pinning down micro-organisms as the cause of many diseases.

# ANAESTHETICS

For hundreds of years, surgical operations were performed quickly to reduce the chances of the patient dying from shock and blood loss. First, the surgeon gave the patient a glug of rum or a dose of opium. Then, they were handed a piece of wood or leather to bite on as they experienced the unimaginable pain of flesh being sliced and bones being sawn.

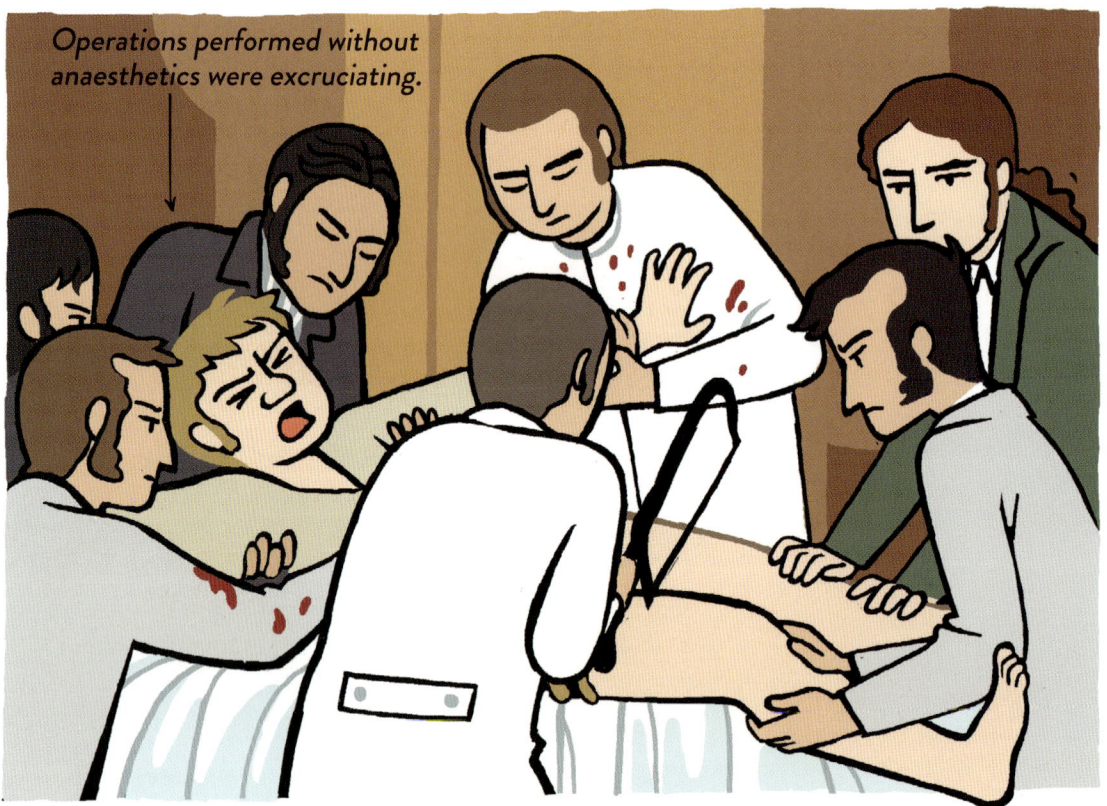

*Operations performed without anaesthetics were excruciating.*

The use of plant-based concoctions to make people unconsciousness had been known in many cultures, including Japan and the Islamic world. Paracelsus (see pages 10–11) discovered the pain-relieving properties of diethyl ether in the 1520s. By the 1820s, Western chemists had also produced pain-relieving gases such as nitrous oxide, also known as laughing gas.

Ether was first used medically in 1842 by American medical student William Clarke (1819–1908), who anaesthetised a patient for a tooth extraction, and doctor Crawford Long (1815–78), who removed a tumour from a patient's neck while using ether. In October 1846 American dentist William Morton (1819–68) publicly demonstrated the use of the anaesthetic at Massachusetts General Hospital, Boston, USA. Gradually the idea of using anaesthetics during surgery caught on.

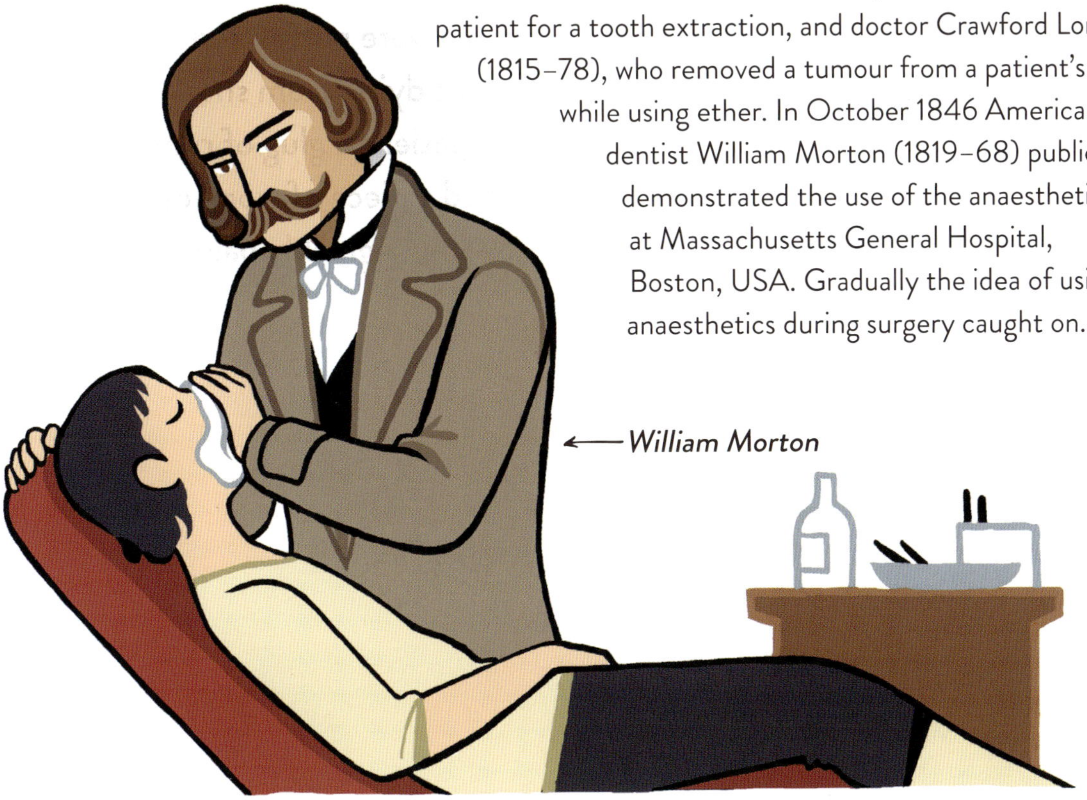

← *William Morton*

## Royal Approval

In Europe, Scottish doctor James Simpson (1811–70) first used the chemical chloroform as an anaesthetic in 1847. Chloroform was given by dripping it onto a cloth mask until the patient lost consciousness. The ultimate seal of approval for the use of anaesthetics in the United Kingdom occurred in 1853, when John Snow (see pages 20–21) was invited to give pain-relieving chloroform to Queen Victoria (1819–1901) during the birth of her eighth child.

*Queen Victoria*

# LOUIS PASTEUR AND VACCINES

The pioneering work of French biologist Louis Pasteur (1822–95) helped to prove once and for all that micro-organisms cause illnesses. Pasteur also made key discoveries in the field of vaccination, helping to protect millions against deadly diseases.

In 1856 Pasteur was asked to investigate the process of fermentation in the wine industry. He proved that fermentation was caused by yeast, which converts sugars into alcohol. He also discovered that heating liquids, such as milk, to between 60 and 100 degrees kills the micro-organisms that cause it to spoil – a process that became known as 'pasteurisation'.

Pasteur suspected that the micro-organisms that cause food to go off also caused diseases and infections in the human body. The paper he wrote on this was read by Sir Joseph Lister (1827–1912), leading to his methods of antiseptic surgery (see pages 26–27).

Louis Pasteur

Later in his career, Pasteur proved that vaccines made from a weakened version of disease-causing micro-organisms, when injected into someone, made them immune to the deadly form of the disease. He tested this in 1885 when he created the first vaccine against the viral disease rabies. Nearly always fatal, rabies affects the nervous system, causing the victim's brain to swell and producing agonisingly painful muscle spasms.

Pasteur supervised the injection of his rabies vaccine into a nine-year-old boy who had been mauled by an infected dog. The boy didn't develop the disease. By the end of the next year 350 people had been treated with Pasteur's vaccine. This research led the way to developing further vaccines against diseases that had killed millions throughout history.

*Rabies is so severe that a rabid dog goes mad with pain.*

# ANTISEPTIC SURGERY

Before about 1860, hospital instruments and operating tables weren't properly cleaned, surgeons didn't wear face masks and operated in filthy, blood-splattered gowns. Theatre floors were slippery with gore from the day's previous patients and surviving surgery was a matter of luck.

English surgeon Joseph Lister was inspired by Pasteur's work on micro-organisms (see pages 24–25). Lister wondered if micro-organisms were also to blame for hospital infections. He began to experiment with carbolic acid, which was strongly antiseptic. Lister sprayed it in the air during operations, applied it to bandages, swabbed it on wounds and instructed his staff to wear clean gowns and wash their hands. Infection rates fell and many more patients survived operations.

← *A carbolic spray apparatus in use during an operation*

Lister published his findings in 1869 and his ideas began to spread. Although his critics mocked him at first, by the end of the century antiseptic surgery was accepted as the norm.

Joseph Lister

## Florence Nightingale

The work of Florence Nightingale (1820-1910) revolutionised nursing care in the mid 19th century. Before Nightingale's work, which began in an army hospital during the Crimean War (1853–56), nurses were often uneducated and poorly trained; as a result, hospitals had low standards of hygiene and patient care.

At a time when women were not encouraged to work outside the home, Nightingale established a professional nursing school for women, promoted the spread of medical knowledge and encouraged the idea of women entering the workplace.

Florence Nightingale

# PSYCHIATRY

Before the 20th century the workings of the human mind were poorly understood. Pioneering doctors, such as Austrian Sigmund Freud (1856–1939), gradually developed a new area of medicine – psychiatry – to try to understand what triggers mental illness.

In the past, many people suffering from diseases of the mind were often treated with great cruelty. Labelled 'lunatics' – as their symptoms were thought to be influenced by the Moon, or *luna* in Latin – the mentally ill were shut away in grim hospitals called asylums.

*At the beginning of the 19th century, the mentally ill were locked away and restrained in 'mad houses'.*

Patients who were violent or self-harming could be confined in chains and subjected to extreme and degrading 'treatments', such as repeated cold-water drenching. As late as the 1960s 'psychosurgeons' legally performed lobotomies, in which a sharp steel instrument was thrust into the front lobe of a patient's brain, destroying tissue and turning the subject into a passive, easy to manage zombie.

⟵ *A sharp-pointed orbitoclast (pick) and hammer were the tools used to perform lobotomies.*

Treatment of vulnerable patients began to change when doctors made an effort to understand the causes of mental illnesses. Sigmund Freud trained as a specialist in diseases of the nervous system. In the late 19th century Freud gradually developed the science of 'psychoanalysis' by delving deeply into how the unconscious mind affects behaviour. He theorised that influences such as traumatic experiences, compulsive actions, repressed sexual desire, self-loathing and guilt all play their parts in diseases of the mind.

Although highly controversial at the time, Freud's work still influences psychiatrists today as they attempt to understand and compassionately manage the many forms of mental illness.

*Sigmund Freud*

# RÖNTGEN AND X-RAYS

The discovery of X-rays by Wilhelm Röntgen (1845–1923), allowed people to see images of bones and structures within the human body without surgery for the first time. This led to quicker and more accurate diagnoses of injuries and diseases.

Born in Prussia – now part of Germany – Röntgen became a physicist. In 1895, while working at the University of Würzburg, Röntgen was investigating the properties of various types of vacuum tubes. These devices consist of electrodes inside a glass tube from which the air has been removed. When an electric current is passed through them, the tubes give off various forms of radiation, such as light or heat.

*Wilhelm Röntgen* ⟶

While conducting his experiments, Röntgen noticed that a nearby protective screen painted with the chemical barium platinocyanide glowed in the dark when electricity was passed through a certain type of tube. He suspected that a new kind of radiation might be responsible. He called these 'x' rays (in mathematics 'x' represents something unknown). Investigating further, Röntgen saw the faint image of his own skeleton on the screen as the rays passed through him.

Röntgen worked non-stop on his new discovery, eating and sleeping in his laboratory. Two weeks later he took the world's first X-ray picture of the bones in his wife Anna's hand. On seeing the image, Anna is said to have exclaimed, 'I have seen my death!'. Röntgen later produced clearer images of a friend's hand at a public lecture. He is recognised today as the founder of medical imaging.

## Shadow Pictures

Röntgen and many others quickly saw uses for 'shadow pictures'. In 1896, English surgeon John Hall-Edwards used X-rays to help him perform an operation. By 1900 inventors, including American Thomas Edison, had developed 'live imaging' X-ray devices that displayed the body's structures on a screen.

What people didn't realise for some time was that working with X-rays carried enormous risks. Exposed to large doses of unshielded radiation, doctors and scientists suffered skin burns and hair loss. One of Edison's assistants developed an aggressive cancer that killed him in 1904.

*X-ray of Anna Röntgen's hand. Her ring appears solid because the X-rays could not pass through it.*

# MAGIC BULLETS

In the late 19th century, German scientist Paul Ehrlich (1854–1915) dreamed of finding a 'magic bullet' to cure diseases. His groundbreaking work in the fields of cellular biology and drug creation resulted in the first effective treatment for syphilis (see pages 10–11) and laid the foundations of modern cancer chemotherapy.

Paul Ehrlich became an expert at cell staining. The practice of staining microscopic samples with coloured chemicals in order to examine them more accurately under a microscope began in the 1870s. It allowed researchers to identify different types of human cells and to study micro-organisms, such as bacteria, in much greater detail. Ehrlich was able to identify certain types of blood cells for the first time, allowing doctors to diagnose blood diseases.

Ehrlich was invited by respected German biologist Robert Koch (1843–1910) to join his Institute of Infectious Diseases in Berlin in 1891. Drawing on his groundwork in staining, Ehrlich speculated that some chemicals could have targeted toxic effects, both on disease-causing micro-organisms and on cancers. He called these 'magic bullets' – agents that wiped out the disease, but allowed the patient to survive.

*A 19th century microscope*

*Stained human cells*

In 1909 Ehrlich and his assistant, Japanese biologist Sahachiro Hata (1873–1938), developed the drug arsphenamine. This killed the bacteria that caused syphilis, which had been responsible for millions of deaths.

*Paul Ehrlich*

*Sahachiro Hata holds a vial (glass container) of arsphenamine*

## Poisonous Pants

The only previous treatment for syphilis had been mercury, sometimes delivered via coated underpants, which eased the disease's painful symptoms, but eventually poisoned the patient. Arsphenamine became the most effective treatment for syphilis until antibiotics appeared in the 1940s.

# ANTIBIOTICS – A CHANCE DISCOVERY

A chance event in his laboratory led Scottish doctor Alexander Fleming (1881–1955) to discover the antibiotic penicillin.

Before Fleming's discovery, the work of Pasteur, Koch and Ehrlich had highlighted the role of bacteria in causing infections and diseases, but doctors were relatively powerless to stop their growth. This meant that people could die – and often did – from a simple cut. Untreated, a wound could progress from soreness to a massive infection, leading to sepsis – 'blood poisoning' as it was known – and a painful death.

During the First World War (1914–18) Fleming served in battlefield hospitals. He saw that antiseptic chemicals, used by doctors to treat injuries, seemed to have little effect on the infections from which many soldiers died. He suspected, correctly, that these infections were too deep and beyond the reach of surface antiseptics. What was needed was a powerful antibacterial agent that would treat the entire body.

*A First World War field hospital*

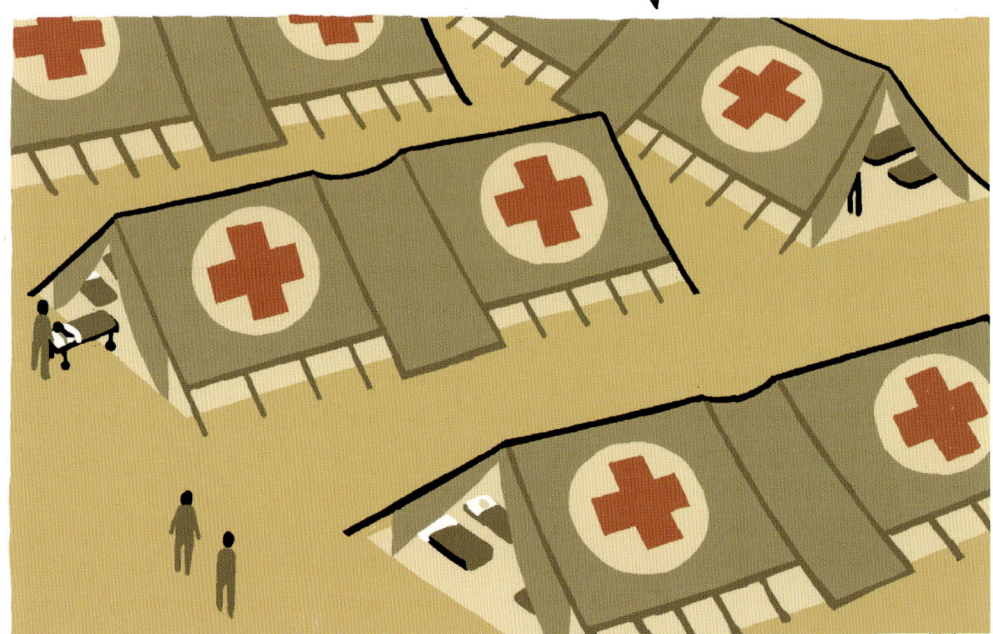

After the war, Fleming continued his research. Returning from holiday in 1928, he found a mouldy dish of bacterial culture in his laboratory. He was surprised to discover that some of the bacteria in this dish had been wiped out by the mould. Fleming isolated the antibiotic agent in the mould and found that it killed bacteria responsible for many common diseases and infections. He had discovered the world's first antibiotic, penicillin.

*Alexander Fleming*

## Mass Production

Fleming published his research in 1929, but little attention was paid to it. With the start of the Second World War (1939–45), however, British and US government funding allowed researchers, such as Howard Florey (1898–1968) and Ernst Chain (1906–79) in Oxford to work out how to mass-produce the drug. By June 1944 there was enough penicillin to treat all the wounded Allied soldiers. When it was eventually manufactured on a larger scale, penicillin revolutionised medicine around the world.

# INSULIN

Before the 1920s, being diagnosed with the disease diabetes was a death sentence. That changed when a team of Canadian researchers, led by orthopaedic (bone) surgeon Frederick Banting (1891–1941), discovered the hormone insulin.

James Collip

Charles Best

## Sugar Levels

Diabetes occurs when the body fails to control its blood sugar levels with the hormone insulin, which is produced in a gland called the pancreas. There are two types of diabetes: type 1 and type 2. In type 1 diabetes the body attacks and destroys the cells that produce insulin; in type 2 diabetes the insulin cells don't work properly.

In both types of diabetes, glucose (sugar obtained from food) is excreted in urine rather than reaching the cells where it is needed. Over time, raised blood sugar levels damage the heart and kidneys. They can also cause blood circulation problems in the feet, leading to amputation; and eye damage, leading to blindness.

*Frederick Banting*

*John Macleod*

Diabetes cannot be cured, but it can be controlled with insulin injections or tablets. In 1921 Frederick Banting, working with Charles Best (1899–1978) and John Macleod (1876–1935) at the University of Toronto, managed to isolate insulin from the pancreas of a dog and inject it into another diabetic animal, whose blood sugar levels returned to normal.

Trials on human subjects proved successful after biochemist James Collip (1892–1965) joined the team and worked out how to produce purified insulin in useful quantities.

Banting and Macleod were awarded the Nobel Prize in 1923 for their work on insulin; they shared the award with Best and Collip. Working together, these four men had changed the lives of diabetes sufferers forever.

# FIRST HEART TRANSPLANT

In the 1960s, there was little that could be done for people with severe heart disease. Then, in 1967, pioneering South African surgeon Christiaan Barnard (1922–2001) performed the world's first successful heart transplant.

Although organ transplant surgery had been performed before – the first kidney transplant had taken place in 1953 – replacing a diseased human heart with one from a dead donor meant that the operation remained the stuff of science fiction. In 1964, Mississippi surgeon James Hardy (1918–2003) transplanted a chimpanzee's heart into a dying man, Boyd Rush (1895–1964). The heart beat for up to 90 minutes, after which Rush died. The operation was criticised by many of his fellow surgeons as unethical and immoral.

← *Christiaan Barnard*

Christiaan Barnard was fascinated by the possibility of heart transplants. In the mid-1960s he began transplanting the hearts of dogs. Although many of Barnard's canine subjects only lived for a few days with their transplanted hearts, by 1967 he felt ready to try the procedure on a human.

On 3 December 1967 Barnard transplanted the heart of a young woman, who had been left brain-dead by a road traffic accident, into the chest of a 54-year-old man, Louis Washkansky (1913–67). The operation took five hours. Washkansky lived for 18 days, but eventually died of pneumonia. In the next few years Barnard performed many more heart transplants. Survival times improved; one patient lived more than 23 years with his new heart. Today the procedure saves up to 3,500 lives every year.

Louis Washkansky ⟶

## New Developments

Two medical developments helped make the operation possible. The first was the heart-lung machine that pumped blood around the patient, giving surgeons time to remove the diseased heart and sew the new donor heart into place. The second was the development of effective immuno-suppressant drugs, which prevent the patient's body from rejecting the new organ.

# IMAGING

Since the mid-20th century doctors have been able to image the structures inside the human body in ever-greater levels of detail. Whether checking the health of an unborn baby or revealing problems, such as blood clots, heart disease and tumours, imaging is now an essential part of medicine worldwide.

Ultrasound uses harmless high-frequency waves of sound to create pictures. In 1794, Italian biologist Lazzaro Spallanzani (1729–99) first discovered that bats use sound to find their way and prey in the dark. This discovery eventually led scientists during the First World War to develop 'echolocation' to try and pinpoint enemy submarines.

*Lazzaro Spallanzani*

*A bat uses echolocation to hunt prey*

In 1942 Austrian neurologist Karl Dussik (1908–68) first used sound waves to try to detect brain tumours. In the 1980s ultrasonic equipment had advanced to the stage where sound waves were able to create 3D pictures of body structures, and by the 1990s real-time ultrasound had arrived to guide surgeons during operations.

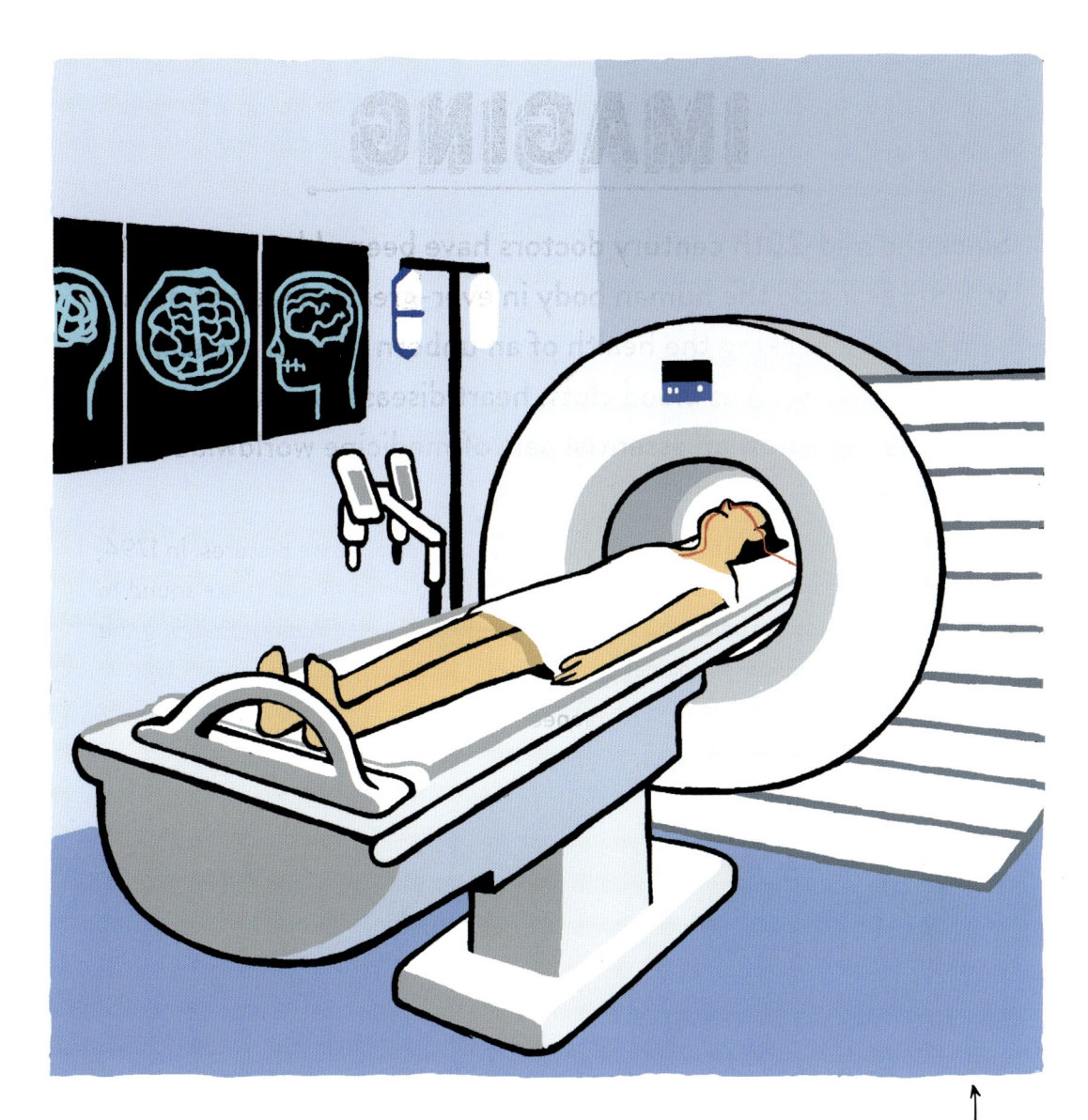

*A CT scanner*

CT (computerised tomography) scanning uses X-rays to produce 'slices' through the body, building up a detailed picture of what's inside. The technology was first developed by English engineer Godfrey Hounsfield (1919–2004) and South African American physicist Allan Cormack (1924–98) in 1972.

At first, it was used for head-only imaging. Later, CT scanning machines were enlarged to allow body scans. As computing power increased hugely throughout the later 20th century, CT scans became faster and much more detailed. The first CT images took days to produce; today a detailed chest scan can be completed in around 10 seconds.

# JOINT REPLACEMENT SURGERY

The hips and knees are two of the most important joints in the human skeleton. However, they can be damaged through trauma, such as falls or accidents, or they can simply wear out with age, causing pain and stiffness.

A key moment in 20th century medicine was the development of joint replacement surgery. Once pioneering procedures, today joint replacements are now some of the most commonly performed operations. Replacement joints, or prostheses (singular prosthesis), have improved dramatically and are now made from super-strong, lightweight metals, such as titanium.

Attempts to replace hips go as far back as Germany in 1891. Brilliant English surgeon Sir John Charnley (1911–82) refined the operation in the early 1960s, designing a new form of prosthesis made from stainless steel, which rotated in a tough plastic cup.

*Sir John Charnley holding an artificial hip joint*

Charnley also hugely improved the operation's success rate. After experiencing unacceptable levels of nasty post-operative infections in his patients, Charnley worked with a manufacturer to design and build a special operating theatre air filtration system. This helped prevent bacteria from entering the exposed hip joint during the operation. He also designed an operating 'space suit' for the surgeon, which was sealed and came with its own cooled air supply.

*Surgeons operating while wearing surgical 'space suits'*

# New Knees

Knee replacement, or knee arthroplasty, involves cutting open the knee and replacing its weight-bearing components with metal and plastic implants, sometimes replacing the end of the femur as well. First performed in 1968 and refined ever since, knee replacements now account for up to five per cent of all operations performed in the US.

# GENETIC THERAPY AND THE FUTURE

First proposed in the 1970s, genetic therapy, or the ability to cure an inherited disease by altering the faulty genes that cause it, has become an important area of medical research. Genetic therapy may hold the key to curing some currently incurable diseases.

Inherited from our parents, genes determine our physical characteristics, such as hair colour and how tall we grow. Genes are made up of DNA (deoxyribonucleic acid), which is a sequence of pairs of molecules. These twist together in a 'double helix' shape – rather like a microscopic twisty ladder. This discovery was the work of four brilliant scientists: Francis Crick (1916–2004), Rosalind Franklin (1920–58), James Watson (1928–) and Maurice Wilkins (1916–2004).

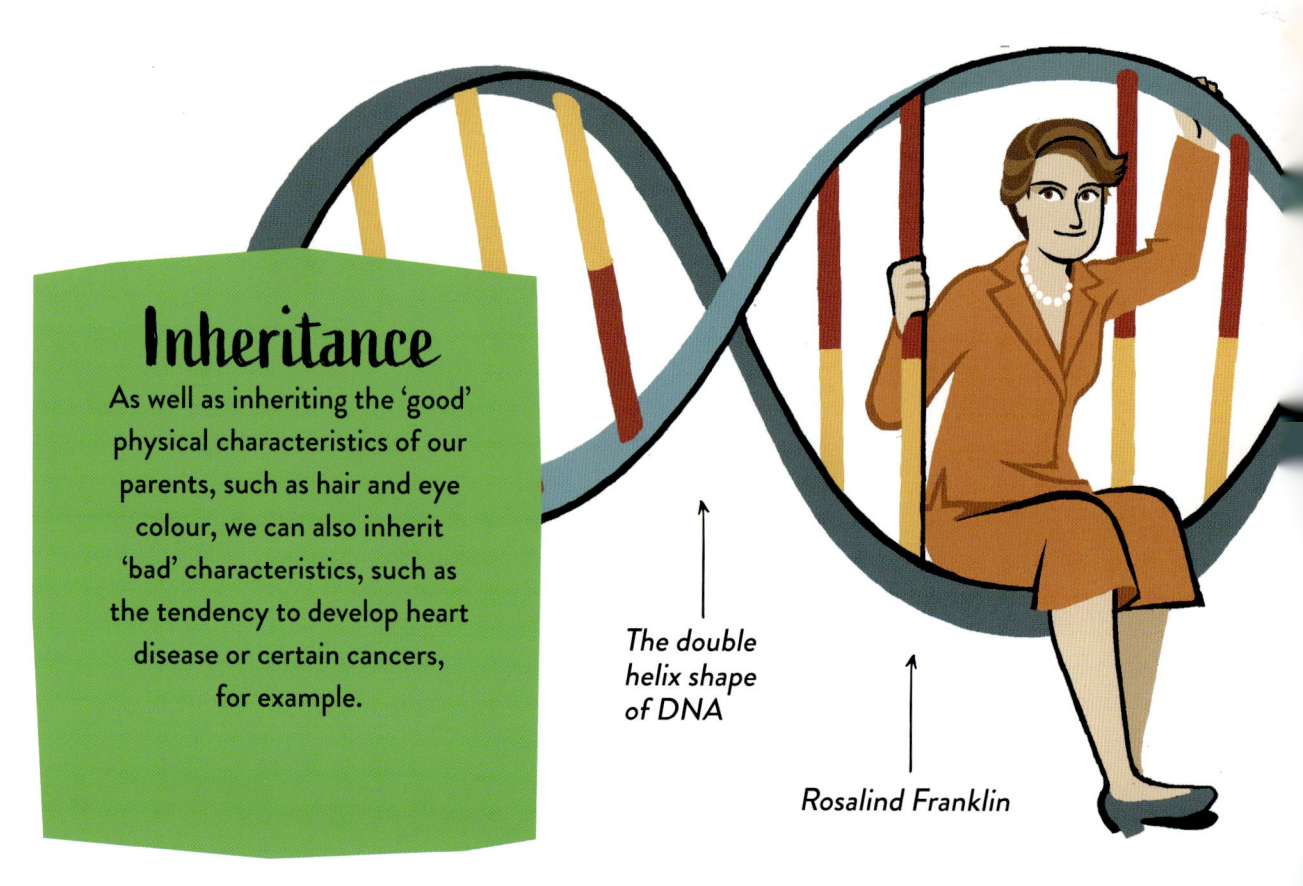

## Inheritance

As well as inheriting the 'good' physical characteristics of our parents, such as hair and eye colour, we can also inherit 'bad' characteristics, such as the tendency to develop heart disease or certain cancers, for example.

*The double helix shape of DNA*

*Rosalind Franklin*

Gene therapy aims to replace faulty genes with healthy ones. One way of doing this is to introduce modified genes into the body via a virus. Viruses normally attack the body by injecting their DNA into healthy cells. However, researchers can modify a virus to carry healthy genetic material. The problem is that, just as the body's immune system repels the nasty viruses attacking it, 'good' viruses might also be wiped out.

*From left to right: Maurice Wilkins, Francis Crick, James Watson. They were awarded the Nobel Prize for their discovery. Franklin's vital contribution was not recognised until after her death.*

Although predictions about the future are usually unreliable, one thing is certain in the world of medicine – there will always be new challenges for scientists and doctors to overcome. In recent years, medicine has had to quickly respond to previously unknown viruses, such as Ebola and SARS-Cov-2 (the COVID-19 coronavirus). Given the rapid advances of the last two hundred years, who knows what will be accomplished in the future?

# GLOSSARY

**acupuncture** In Chinese medicine, inserting fine needles into the body to balance energy flow
**agent** Something that performs an action
**Allied** The countries, such as Britain and the US, that fought against the Nazis in the Second World War
**amputation** Cutting off an arm or leg
**anaesthetic** A chemical or drug that causes a patient to temporarily lose consciousness and feel no pain
**anatomy** Studying the parts of the body
**antibiotic** A drug that kills bacteria inside the body
**antiseptic** A substance that kills bacteria on surfaces
**bacterium** (plural bacteria) A micro-organism that can cause disease
**biology** The study of living things
**cell** A tiny structure within the human body, from which all larger structures, such as organs or bones, are made
**cesspit** A pit where sewage or liquid waste is kept
**circulation** To flow in a loop
**dissect** To cut up or cut open a body
**electrode** Something that releases electricity
**germ** Something that causes disease
**heart-lung machine** A machine that takes over the work of the heart and lungs during an operation
**immune system** The body system that resists infections and toxins
**inoculation** To deliberately give someone a mild disease in order to prevent a more serious related disease
**Islamic** Relating to Islam, the religion of Muslims
**lobe** Part of a body structure, such as the brain
**micro-organism** A living thing, such as a bacterium or virus, too small to be seen by the naked eye
**Nobel Prize** A large international cash prize awarded for outstanding work in fields, such as medicine, science or literature
**osteoarthritis** Pain caused by wear and tear on body joints

**prosthesis** A replacement body part made from artificial materials
**psychiatry** The science (and study and treatment) of how the mind affects our behaviour
**radiation** Waves of energy, such as heat or light, emitted from something
**sacrifice** To kill something living to please a god or gods
**toxic** Poisonous
**transplant** To replace one body part with another from a human donor
**trauma** A damaging event, such as an accident or battle wound
**tumour** An unnatural cell growth in the body that produces a lump of tissue
**ultrasound** High-frequency sound waves used to image structures within the body
**vaccination** To create a vaccine from a weakened form of a disease that, when injected, protects the patient from getting that disease
**virus** A micro-organism that is smaller than a bacterium and spreads by injecting its DNA into healthy cells
**vitamin** An essential substance we get from our food, such as vitamin C

# FURTHER INFORMATION

## Books

*10 Ideas That Changed the World*
by Cath Senker (Wayland, 2015)

*All That Matters: A History of Medicine*
by Tim Hall (John Murray, 2013)

*The Bright and Bold Human Body* (series)
by Izzi Howell (Wayland, 2020)

*Florence Nightingale:*
*Social Reformer and Pioneer of Nursing*
by Sarah Ridley (Franklin Watts, 2020)

*Future Science Now!:*
*What's Next For Medicine?*
by Tom Jackson (Wayland, 2015)

*The Grisly History of Medicine:* (series)
by John Farndon (Hungry Tomato, 2017)

*Operation Ouch!:*
*Medical Milestones and Crazy Cures*
by Chris van Tulleken (Little, Brown Books for Young Readers, 2014)

Note to parents and teachers: Every effort has been made by the Publishers to ensure that the websites in this book are of the highest educational value, and that they contain no inappropriate or offensive material. However, because of the nature of the Internet, it is impossible to guarantee that the contents of these sites will not be altered. We strongly advise that Internet access is supervised by a responsible adult.

## Websites

www.bbc.co.uk/bitesize/guides/zxg6wxs/revision/1
A BBC timeline on the history of medicine

www.gosh.org/what-we-do/research/breakthroughs-childrens-medicine/heart-and-lung-breakthrough-guide
These interactive guides by The Great Ormond Street Hospital cover the history and breakthroughs in many medical fields, such as heart and lung surgery, cancer and genetics.

www.wellcomecollection.org
The web portal of the Wellcome Collection in London, with stories and information on their medicine-related exhibitions

www.rcseng.ac.uk/museums-and-archives/hunterian-museum/
The website of the Hunterian Museum of the Royal College of Surgeons, London

www.si.edu
The web portal of the Smithsonian. Type in 'medicine' to search content related to the history of medicine.

www.knowitall.org/document/history-medicine-kids-work
The medical history section of a US children's general knowledge website

http://encyclopedia.kids.net.au/page/hi/History_of_medicine
The medical history section of an Australian children's general knowledge website

## Places to visit

The Hunterian
Glasgow G12 8QQ
www.gla.ac.uk/hunterian/
collections/permanentdisplays/
hunterianmuseum/

Bethlem Muesum of the Mind
Kent BR3 3BX
www.museumofthemind.org.uk

Old Operating Theatre Museum
London SE1 9RY
www.oldoperatingtheatre.com

George Marshall Medical Museum
Worcester WR5 1DD
www.medicalmuseum.org.uk

Alexander Fleming Lab Museum
London W2 1NY
www.medicalmuseums.org/
museums/alex.htm

Science Museum
London SW7 2DD
www.sciencemuseum.org.uk/

Thackray Medical Museum
Leeds LS9 7LN
www.thackraymedicalmuseum.co.uk

Wellcome Collection
London NW1 2BE
www.wellcomecollection.org

# INDEX

air 6, 7, 20, 26, 30, 43
anatomy 7, 12–13
animals 4, 7, 12, 13, 15
Anson, Admiral George 16
antibiotics 33, 34–35
antisepsis 11, 24, 26–27, 34

bacteria 20, 32, 33, 34, 35, 43
Banting, Frederick 36, 37
Barnard, Christiaan 38, 39
blood 6, 7, 11, 14–15, 22, 32, 34, 36, 37, 39, 40
bones 4, 5, 12, 22, 30, 31, 36
books 8, 9, 13, 14

cancer 31, 32, 44
cells 32, 36, 37, 45
Charles Best 36, 37
Charnley, Sir John 42, 43
China 8, 9, 18
Clarke, William 23
Collip, James 36, 37
Cormack, Allan 41
Crick, Francis 44, 45

diabetes 36–37
dissection 7, 12–13, 15
DNA 44, 45
drugs (medicinal) 11, 32, 33, 35, 39
    arsphenamine 33

Edison, Thomas 31
Ehrlich, Paul 32, 33, 34
epidemics 18, 20

First World War 34, 35, 40
Fleming, Alexander 34, 35
Franklin, Rosalind 44, 45
Freud, Sigmund 28, 29

Galenus, Aelius (Galen) 7, 10, 12, 13, 15
genes 44–45
germs 18, 20

Hardy, James 38
Harvey, William 14, 15
Hata, Sahachiro 33
heart 14, 15, 37, 38, 39
heart disease 38, 39, 40, 44
Hippocrates 6, 10
Hounsfield, Godfrey 41
Huangdi (The Yellow Emperor) 8
humours 6, 7, 10

immune system 18, 19, 25, 45
Islamic world 8–9, 22

Jenner, Edward 18, 19

kidneys 16, 37, 38
Koch, Robert 32, 34

Lind, James 16, 17
Lister, Sir Joseph 24, 26–27
Long, Crawford 23
lungs 15, 39

Macleod, John 36, 37
mental illness 28–29
micro-organisms 21, 24, 25, 26, 32
Morton, William 23
muscles 12, 13, 25

Nightingale, Florence 27
Nobel Prize 37, 45

opium 11, 22
Oporinus, Johannes 13
organs 12, 13, 38, 39

Paracelsus 10, 11, 22
Pasteur, Louis 24–25, 26, 34
Phipps, James 19
plants 4, 7, 8, 11, 22

Queen Victoria 23

rabies 24
radiation 30
Rush, Boyd 38
Röntgen, Anna 31
Röntgen, Wilhelm 30

Second World War 35
sepsis 34
Simpson, James 23
Sīnā, Ibn (Avicenna) 9
skeleton 13, 31, 42
Snow, John 20, 21, 23
Spallanzani, Lazzaro 40
surgery 5, 7, 12, 23, 24, 26–27, 30, 38, 42–43
syphilis 11, 32, 33

transplants 38, 39
Turkey 7, 18

vaccination 18, 19, 24, 25
Vesalius, Andreas 12
virus 18, 45
von Hohenheim, Theophrastus Bombastus (see Paracelsus)

Washkansky, Louis 39
Watson, James 44, 45
Wilkins, Maurice 44, 45

X-rays 41